warmest wishes
dear Lucy
for reading
Jane
X

Eve Said

Jane Wilkinson is a British-Irish poet currently living in Norwich. She has lived in Manchester and for many years, in London, where she studied Fine Art, went on to work in arts administration and trained and practised as a Landscape Architect. She has published widely in journals, including *The Rialto Magazine, Under the Radar, The Lighthouse Literary Journal, Ink Sweat and Tears, Alchemy Spoon* and *Magma*. She has won the Aesthetica Poetry Prize (2022), the Manchester Poetry Prize (2022), Hamish Canham Prize (2021), Guernsey Literary Festival Poetry Prize (2020), Strokestown Poetry Festival Prize (2022), Against the Grain Poetry Perss Prize (2019), Morley Poetry Competition (2019) and been longlisted in the National Poetry Competition. This is her debut collection, selected as a winner of the Live Canon 2022 Collection Competition.

First Published in 2023

by Live Canon Poetry Ltd
www.livecanon.co.uk

All rights reserved

© Jane Wilkinson

978-1-909703-26-1

Contents

iii.   sons of sons

Acknowledgements

Thank you to the editors of the following publications in which some of these poems first appeared: Fenland Reed issue 8; Lighthouse Literary Journal issue 22; Magma: *Act your Age* issue 77; Live Canon anthology *(More) new poems for Christmas*; Dempsey and Windle anthology *Horses of a different colour*; Emma Press anthology *Everything that can happen: poems about the future.*

'Kingfisher' received third prize in the Brian Dempsey Memorial Competition, 2021; 'Angela once said that parenting is immersive' received first prize in the Guernsey Literary Festival Poetry Prize, 2020; 'If I were to land' received first prize in Strokestown Poetry Prize, 2020; 'Diptych' received first prize in the Against the Grain Press Poetry Prize, 2019; 'Lichen!' received second prize and 'Not black at all' was commended in Waltham Forest Poetry Prize, 2018.

I owe a debt of gratitude to those first readers of these poems: to Ros Barber, my first poetry guide, who provided soft landings at the Poetry School; to Sue Burge and Esther Morgan who gracefully midwifed this book and to Julia Webb and the fine members of the Norwich Stanza Group for their inspiration and conversation; thank you to all my writing groups Newham Stanza and Norwich, NPG and the Thursday Groups for your kind attention, close reading and critique. I am also so grateful to Café Writers poetry organisation for their support and nurture.

Thank you to Andrea Holland, Jane Draycott, John Greening, Doug Jones, Ken Evans, Helen Ivory, Sophie Essex, Fiona Sampson, Anna Cathenka, Deryn Rees-Jones and George Szirtes, who all said or did the right thing at the right time, and to all the wonderful poets and dear friends with whom I have travelled. A huge thank you to Live Canon and Susannah Hart for selecting *Eve said* for publication. To Paul and Gabriel, thank you isn't enough.

1. Eve said

Eve said

yes, we stewed them, froze them, parcelled up and dispensed them crammed in bags but in the end we were left with two buckets and the large red trug, filled with windfall overwhelm, which in turn flooded. The golden apples floated: half in, half-waterlogged bodies in a rainbath. As time passed, they took my attention as they should not have. Some reacted black. How do they oxidise? How long does the cartilage core hold out, hold on to the heart locket, keep safe the apple-seed tears? Will we go custard soft, all cidery rot tanked in the earth like these apple coffins? Birds flocked to the apple bobbing. The blackbird couple relished the strange storage; jittery bright-eyed jewellers tilting one thick lens to inspect each bauble, their bulky balance gave them the edge. The inedible pears though... monstrous desiccated fists – Eve whispered this into her hand as if He were listening – so feral, even the juice is foul, abruptly separating ghastly as bone stock; still, their half-buried freckled skulls make excellent worm fodder.

Blood

The Odalisque's unassailable half-draped thighs
are bloodless as soft white loaves; on the opposite

gallery wall St. Lucy carries her eyes on a plate,
lidded and staring at me like dead fish do, the wit

of their body left at sea. Sometimes I'm surprised
how red the toilet water turns, how gently I can

cup my own head, how quietly hair grows.
Discovering how blood flows, my son presses

down to stopper a vein on the back of my hand,
then plays the tendons in the wrist, my body sings

the memory of making the self-same gesture.
A jackdaw boy couldn't fly, the jackdaw mother

circled until night. Whimpering in the long grass
his gaping yellow craw finally became a target.

Defenceless as raw eggs my eyes break open
let the morning light glance on ungathered tears.

The nine benefits of crying
from the Book of Lists

you weigh out your emotions in flour and salt,
I try to reverse the equation of water

after the deluge is a time of purification; I mop up
the flood by hand, bitter tears redeem

my body is left numb, holding a blue-glass eye bath
and a prescription for oxytocin

the way mist crawls in, too atomised to be tangible,
how can we, unaccompanied, staunch the flow?

simple as diagrams of molecules, we are all chemical,
in our unbreached bonds to one another

people drip by in the street, in the park, on fragile rafts,
trickles of couples, small floating families

I stand there dissolving, looking up with cathedral eyes
in the vanquished light

imagine how you cried once before, they say,
to clear the lungs of fluid

the long night is marine, water never sleeps and we
are mostly water; cry yourself quiet

Diurnal moon

Whispered confidences,
like fish under glass,
dart quick then stop.
I think I saw the pink
hint of watery blood

tint the root
of this afternoon's half
moon – expectant.

Her convex shore is blurred.
She is a button pushed halfway
through the buttonhole
of a sky-blue shirt.
Both of us are undressing.

His echoed heart
is gone. Tell the moon
the ultrasound is mute.

Things best done slowly
from the Book of Lists

Measuring and weighing out ingredients.
Falling over when he's there to catch your fall.

Growing up. That is to say growing into,
naming stars, naming plants, naming children,

splitting eggs, shelling peas, counting mulberries.
Injecting subcutaneously to make a boy.

I make war
                    with March then tie myself
to the bedhead. Wired writhing comes
and goes, patchworked with pleas. I am a gate
banging in the wind, its crude latch knotted
with tendons of love. I – as in we –
fire up again. Contractions. 'Thank you bed,
for being here, concrete.' I cry things in my
head; make the flat sound of a cracked cup.
Yes, I had named him. This last day
is a tornado. Finally I wobble out
of my earthhole, filthy and dried-blood nails.
In the bathroom I lay a skinned egg,
black and red, about the size of my heart.

26 possible ways in which I don't make a self-portrait
from the Book of Lists

By using only the medium of exhaled smoke.

Through extreme photographic under-exposure.

By repeatedly tracing a drawing until all descriptive detail is defaced.

In representing only negative space.

Dressed in disguise so as to be you, dear reader

pictured, completely obscured behind a door.

As a bee in Cranach's painting of Cupid's complaint.

As the dialling tone, in a piece of Fluxus Sound Art.

As a fragment of my fingerprint left in a handmade copy of a porcelain
        sunflower seed, made to replace one stolen from Ai Wei Wei's
                            Tate Modern installation.

As a grainy face at an attic window pane.

By concealing it in a chrome-yellow hand bag, used in a Dalston
                            streetwear shoot.

By wanting it to be beautiful.

In the illumination offered by a glint of sunlight glancing off
                    the crest of a small grey wave in the Thames estuary.

Through elusive and momentary ignitions of self-possession.

In a pure white spherical plum-sized pebble, found in a dried-up stream.

In the constricted, red velvet cinema of your recurring sex dreams.

As the small, secretive, predominately brown female of the species
                     Polyommatus icarus or Common Blue butterfly.

In a flattened patch amongst the susurrus of long grass under
                             a mackerel sky.

In the conscious act of carrying a glossy red seed indefinitely
                    in the bottom of a blue rucksack.

As a series of one-minute film clips, called *Strangers Wearing My Hats*.

By sitting very still,

in St. Peter-on-the-Wall, built 625, an isolated marsh chapel.

Drawn in house dust with a finger.

Drawn with a finger on a steamed car window.

In what remains on the page

after a pencil drawing is erased.

Not black at all

She lands distracted, on less than a twig, sleek sky fish, whole
as a doorknob, an unreflecting gouache brushfall laid down
by a troubled hand pausing, repausing for the paint to decide,
where to spill some flight into a bare line of difference between
the field of pigment and its other: white air. Could I even start
to try to concoct *Tan Leather Boot-toe Rubbed Matt With Black*
and then say that, there, that is what her colour was, it comes out
as *Rotten January Acorn*, a lonely sod unloosened between
the toes of some other tree, maybe hornbeam; we walked
and walked, just to find two acorns still fresh enough to qualify
as whole, to bag up, then cast a senseless desperate spell to poultice
our ache, to make our making, make something whole and now
here she is, *Flat Coke* feathers, the fleet glass-bead-eye blackbird
counting out her winter from berry to berry; what future nestfuls.

Pinus coulteri

Percussive seedbomb.
You can play her hundred

Fibonacci scale fingernails
with yours, plink-sing

the bad lullaby of a wind
that bumped her out

of paradise. A full head
of teeth and a *Yes*!

that explodes with self-
sufficient sex. She's swayed

by the rain to flat pack
her porcupine stacks

into a kindling grenade.
Pineapple without its apple,

fleshless fetish object,
with the girth of a shrunken

head. Pinecone. Could I
be your mother tree?

twelve impossible things
from the Book of Lists

Take care of yourself.

Take three strands of pearls daily with a Martini.

Acknowledge your feelings.

Implore one offshore wind turbine
to reverse the weather.

Understand your options.

Find two approachable swans looking for love
in perpetual winter mornings while the black-haired
trees are still drowsy.

Re-establish intimacy with your partner.

At least four unwrapped executive afternoons were
lost down the back of the sofa; I muffled your ears
in the white noise of my thighs.

Join an infertility support group.

Five is missing.

Learn about the normal responses to infertility.

Snap off the hands of six clocks.

Always be honest with your partner.

Secretly gather a choir of seven whales: he said
their songs have no colour. I can hear the barnacle
clink of lips, brushing accidentally in deep ocean.

Be optimistic — but also realistic.

Imagine eight hours straight dazzled by a baby's face:
time dwindling to pure adornment.

Improve your communication about infertility.

I'd swap my losses for nine years' sacrifice.

Speak with a trusted counsellor.

> Ten daisies bloomed and shrivelled on my
> *broderie anglaise* skirt.

Don't blame yourself.

> Waiting at car park number eleven. I wonder why
> it's never over?

Find healthy outlets for your emotions.

> Twelve white scratches appear: twelve saloon cars
> are furiously keyed.

In vitro

I. Egg retrieval

Born at noon on newsprint, words stuck to me
backwards. I was delivered here, by soothing

voices, muslin straining lamplight. Bring bowls now,
pipettes, featherweight things, bring a slight

air of detachment for catching drips, for draining
fluids, instruments for entering, tools to separate

two million oocytes into curds and whey.
I was born with a nest and a brood intact.

II. Fertilisation

we sat, taut as benefactors
in a panel painting
we knelt, we prayed, or nearly,
by an automatic door, *what if all rooms*
continue to lead to smaller rooms?
when the annunciation came
dispatched from the snow-sterilised lab
(as a deeply chilled bud,
as hieroglyphic bird calls)
it was Sunday morning,
love was locked up
in a long-distance phone call with cell division
in a small plastic box,
the worms were oblivious,
the air was oblivious between us,
all High Office oblivious, an orderly angel
alighted with our version of joy
inscribed on a rib-bone sky,
her huge wings, richly closed curtains
to keep his spinal column warm,
to keep his apple-seed eye quiet

III. Blastocyst

Condense my pared nail-white DNA,
soft as the skin on
a bloodwarm junket,
sweet as vanilla dust and candied stem cells.
Zygote zygote, mulberry morula.

IV. Embryo transfer

On the gallery wall, the lab-white frame is striped with shelves.
Porcelain installation, thin as milk poured out to wafer. Impure
white, jug cup saucer cylinder. Clay thimbles made by dipping
finger in clay slip. Thumbprints on the neck. A bowl is made/
unmade/mended with gold. Kintsugi.

                                        Ungilded I attend his
beginning. A Private View under the whitest light, I'm a cracked
pot, with a chipped rim. Perfectly damaged. Mould his feet from
a pinch of my flesh and silk satin mouth lining. A see-saw stack
of cats' bowls, Georgian small: the stainless trolley wheels off,
quietly as possible, as if the minute handmade man is sleeping.

V. Implantation

             two weeks for the proving and the proof
        await the wildness of yeast
           released into the wilderness of my hot red room

Looking out from the fifth-floor ward

my one last whole thought

drowned in the treacle river water

I saw Big Ben's moon-face

patiently scan St Thomas' curtain walls

saw the first star

pinned on molten blue above the city

and the clock's silver light split

to minnows by the passing boats.

The baby was late.

Time was running out

then there was storm

in my bloodstream.

Please, I said, *I feel fragile*

as a reef.

In the nest of bioluminescent tubes,

a pocketful of oxygen is brought

and you

cold from the five a.m. tube train

from running the November bridge

I breathe *in* and at last, *out.*

The pale green ward at night,

light through water, the beds, islands

with no harbour, somewhere a constant motor whined.

I slept for only seconds
    held his novel weight   a soft haul
and swam out,
lost like plankton in the shadows of coral corridors

    where the mothers wheel their fish tanks,
bewildered, as if we'd birthed pearls in glass shells.

Night feed

my breast is bound
from within
by a thin constricting itch

the foremilk frees
a trembling of finches
a first sweet slake

yields the creamy ounce
in a heartbeat
he lies asleep mouth ajar

our sweat shared out evenly
fringe blown back
in a babbling tunnel

of an almost dream
where he nearly speaks
in suckle and flutter

a prayer of godwits
abandoning his body
to the air

Baby asleep in 1902

after *Baby asleep*, Jacob Epstein (1880 - 1959)

New-born baby you are one hundred and seventeen years old.
Pure white sleep on a pillow shelf, your head, so alone,
is life size, is the size of your mother's still puffy grieving womb.
Perfect puckered chin, lower lip withdrawn to pout a comfort
suckle from inside this bronze caul, the only dreaming witness
to a flaming cauldron in a petrified forest. In the wedge of air
behind the left ear, unseen, nonetheless attentively modelled,
contours are lucid as Holbein's pencil portraits and the right ear
is formed by three strong finger holds pressed tenderly
but as if they'd held a hardening eggshell too long. The metal
is the green-black of a shrivelled umbilical; yours must
have been still tied like a pig's tail to (long since lost) a flesh
body. Zipped-in half-grown eyeballs simmer in their bindings.
You have yet to know the importance of learning how to lie.

Remember whose you are

remember your heart, is a little red
fishing boat, low
in the oily epithelium of the sea,

each wave's brow quietening
under the gull's shadow
under the wreath of this steel evening,

my heelbone leaves a dint,
a hominid memory, incident
of rock and pressure ground to sand,

after comprehensive tests, over seven years;
of sifting, caving, containing
an accumulation, by bucket and by spade

can you believe it? my boy said at last
this grain of sand was a mountain range,
a granulation the tissue

of my plantar fascia is thankful for;
I hope you will remember the felty sky
drawing over this corner

of the North Sea
and all its belongings, the crimson
and coal-black and magenta,

weed hair displayed on the beach
where the sea comes to sleep like a mother
homesick for the shore

Kingfisher

Reclusively glamorous, hipper-than-thou,
escapologist in a cocktail dress slips
the lock of our gaze, dives off the sun's rigging,

a forager in thin seclusion, starstruck,
we watch you nonetheless watching yourself,
skimming the river mirror, as if in a boulevard

shop window, we net a syncopated glimpse,
land your ephemeral scrap of foreign sky
in our mind's eye, it flutters in our mouths

for years, a prayer for your tailored transience;
precision-forged steel jaw, tiny certain acuity,
blue amulet, warding off disintegration,

the sighting, so much more than any sacrifice
can buy, leaves us beautiful in its wake.

Bedroom

The room has waited – is waiting – in detached light, as if
light walked in and chose not to leave, lay down and slept.

The room is dilute. A little fine rain of winter condensation
on the windows, a raised rough patch of white paint flaking

like eczema. Amongst the lessons in dust is the smell
of hair and cotton sheets worn to soft silver. In what way

could you thank him for twenty-five years of wear by hands,
by feet? Two things to note, a gold-framed mirror, a modest

chandelier of barnacled glass and chalky paint, they focus
the sight of your mind's eye. Updraught of the bed being unmade:

the chandelier sways. Hushed furniture. Close meeting of wool,
denim, collars, cuffs. We are not under the water, but we are

submerged, entrusting our skin to each other's hands.
Light now emanates not from the windows but from the bed.

Uncertain consecrations

Maybe in the chapel, maybe in the chapel wall or in the approach to the altar. Maybe in the wood of the chapel door; in kneeling down or in the chapel kneeler; in rows and lines of tiny crossing stitches; a needle puncturing stretched wool; in the, *I do this repeatedly*; in the sound of steps on chapel stone, clicking by like beads or the blind limestone crustaceans swimming up against the congregation's footfall or maybe it is in the small crocus heart, opening lotus-wise under this unready spring, queuing up outside the chapel porch. There are things we feel sure we cannot see, do you agree? the solar gold, emitting from the compound eye of crocus pollen locked in a petal chamber, its cloistered light.

To garden

It could be the gift – at very least, a consequence –
of last summer's disaffections. The garden

was left to its own devices then. It became blurred,
our plans erased, I pulled the blinds in shame

against its lazy vexation. Intermittency of flood
and sun meant on dry days we had darted

like diving birds to the sea; skirting our patch
as if it was a mistake or the council dump.

You left the lawn a sponge of moss; old shrubs
merged; the remnants of my vegetable plot rose

and fell untended. I felt nothing. Imperial
artichokes flowered purple threads; there were

four small potatoes. Each weather births
its nemesis: indeed, any change casts unpredictable

shadows. This Easter week, blossom snows
on well-weeded gravel; I hold the listless rain

responsible and wonder about the ivy-cave,
the view of it newly revealed by your pruning saw.

How is the weather in the robin's nest,
tucked high into its leaf-rafters? The birds

chose well, temperate; like a cavern climate
the variable conditions hardly penetrate

its steady atmosphere. This would be a good place
to store something as precious as an egg or a ring.

Applegate

erasure *Courtauld Gallery text, Adam and Eve: Lucas Cranach the Elder 1526*

partridges

heron

branch

vine   stork

lion

wild boar   horse

foliage

grass

Paradise

catching its reflection

in the pool of water

close

drawing closer

entwined in the serpent

temptation

puts the apple

in Adam's mouth

ii. daughters of daughters

Milkers

       in the tight black field, inside the herd, in live silence
and the last hours of wet space fallen to earth, I find
      my way in quiet gravity, we each of us possess
           our own closed strangeness, each is led like a word
down a new line as yet unsaid. I wade chest high
      through warm weighted facts, twitching hide sheets,
          the belched bale breath and acquiescing mass,
hospitable as sleep and the tender corridors I haunt
      at night within the darkness of my own packed body

Undaughtering
from the Book of Lists

a daughter is a frame
is a ghost story
a daughter is a series of false starts
a polished surface
you can't keep your eyes off her
a daughter is a spluttering engine
a rescue mission
a peer review
this daughter is aflame
is unfinished business

Anatomy of the ear

When I am deaf, will the sea still live in a shell?
Will the shell roll with my arterial songs –
so happy drunk – sea! I hear you helter-skelter

my inner ear, a tumbler's spirit level. But gentle.
Stand me upright. Slosh loose the tinnitus
with submersible lullabies. Vessel to vessel.

Night after night, I'd lie on one side, my small
world, tilted all at sea, swaddled, hot water bottle
to my ear. Crushed aspirin in a gulp of brine.

The smallest bone in the human body is two
by three millimetres – *stapes,* the stirrup, little shrimp –
wedged in like a stone in a crevice.

It transmits by aural mechanics, grind-organ style,
is peculiar as a Monopoly piece, a bracelet
charm, and these things so easily get lost.

Can you still hear the sea in the conch's pink ear,
warming on the window sill? Can you still hear
your own soft body crouching in the attic of a shell?

Daughters

'for I have heard my daughter say she has often dreamed of
unhappiness and waked herself with laughing'
Much Ado About Nothing, William Shakespeare
Act II, Scene 1

Seeds are the daughters of weeds,
they lie sleeping underground. Daisy,
dandelion, clover. Their unhappy

roots force pale fingers between
the grains of soil, demanding water drops
to soothe their thirsty souls, to ignite

the weeds' unwelcome flowers in the lawn.
Each flagrant millimetre petal
a climbing note of blooming laughter.

Spoon talk

I heard that my fabrication
(stainless cradle or whittled wood,
a proper sliver of silver;
a polished server cast with grapevines
or a steel teaspoon of mother's insistence)
can reframe any taste, any flavour.

Take it from me,
the scurf-skimmer soup-meddler,
take these two mirrored question marks,
front and back, reply to my wide open vowels
to sweetness as comforting as sleep, curled up
in the drawer with a litter of blank dolls.

As if I notice how much
you weigh or self-medicate,
how much is doled out or amassed,
O other warm, yielding little mouth,
how unremarkable, how many times
my cool equable tongue kisses yours.

Doll
from the Book of Lists

        in the desert
        her forehead swallowed by light
        still rocking some strings of knotted hair
Doll   open like an unfolded blanket
        coming into focus
Doll   headless
        cradling Blue Cat
        like a mouse not yet coloured in
Doll   on a tangerine
        her hand dipping her ink-well face
        arriving imprecisely
        with pinking shears
        dressed in knee scabs eating herself
Doll   is a rain-stick with shimmering bead sound
        is ironing herself out
        legless on a violet velveteen stool
Doll   is left outside
        is tissue paper her lines are living folds
        is a skinned frog
        wears a dog face
Doll   of the daffodil trumpet
        legs are a wing
        hands buried in soil
        torso thorn-scratched leaf-green sullied
Doll   standing like a mountain

'the camera is an instrument'

Dorothea Lange photographer (1895–1965)

California's backlot landscape,
hot, itchy distances.
The camera angle low.

Dorothea, you must be on your knees,
to accurately frame the claustrophobia
of poverty. I get closer.

Florence grants this intimate
examination. Mother of seven.
Tarnished silver skin.

Well-worn surface of the photo
the texture of vitamin deficiency.
Her face is a web of lines.

Rumours. About desperate
twisting fishes, heaped in buckets,
selling on the market stall.

Cutlery blackens – spoons, a knife –
left wanting for touch or purpose
at the back of the drawer.

Sepia brown ekes out etched lines
and I'm reminded, etching is the art
of what is left behind.

Out of the dark, out of a flap
of breast, flapping sheet of tent,
make-do sleeve of prayer,

out of hands and tongue.
A toddler squints from a timber trunk,
under a foraged branch

each migrant night –
the cost and weight of a tent pole
unbearable in hand.

Florence just sold her car tyres
for food. The photographic plate
is burnt indelibly by the sun.

Diptych

:left-side (Anne.)

Distance – has now become measurable, in the furniture
of the yew tree where squirrels chase like unleashed monkeys

and other small creatures and even smaller ones make
their way over the surfaces of the world; spring is restless.

Later, you pass by the clockwork grasses, a ticking frenzy,
the open mouths, entrances to paths, O they purse

and pursue, their intentions certain as the compass. Haste
is made in beech avenues through paper leaves and quarrels.

Steady, the milk cow's tail keeps time, flicks at her flank;
the muscles cringe, quick then still; oak's feet wring the clay,

a potter's oozing fist. Shy buckled fingers of the ancient plane tree
scrape baby knuckles to make a girl's curls swing; sing.

There is nothing left to do but warm the glowing pearl
in your furled and shaded chambers, in that darkness,

miniature Elizabeth burns. Anne, you unwind. At one o'clock,
one small bell, one small black beetle weaves a clever route

through the milk of collar lace. A blood spider (would have set
your teeth on edge) walks a dotted line around your neck… Cut Here

:right-side (Elizabeth.)

Cut here to draw the curtains of heavy clothes that muffle
(and contain the internal tick) like a complicated yew hedge;

or the yolk-yellow fallen pine needles that draw, then dampen
the visitor's path. At night, you dream your body is immersed: a ship

wrecked with gold barnacles and heavy with the crowd that cling
to and embroider the coarse hinge hair and exposed milk

simplicity of skin, slinky as ermine; to be both armoured
and anchored in eruptions of pearls and silk; complex foam

waves breaking shore. But when did your heart stiffen, my love,
as starch does in the whorls of the neck ruff on which your head

– summation of the known world – balances carefully on its plate,
proximal as Anne? As well as roses do, the thorns wind their way

around the glossy coronation coat – to deflate that flower? No, you just
take a deeper breath, fingering the buds and twisting your rings

you smell spring coming: woodruff and garlic nose the light, strained
through oak and ash crowns, fed by last year's fall. Elizabeth! London

lies down to let you stand upon it. Then processioning, dogged as tide,
it rises to shelter in your stare that spans yet unknown distance.

Lily

after *Eleven A. M.* Edward Hopper (1882-1967)

Apartment buildings are stifling, every
room stuffed airless like a head cold.
From my mountainous bed I saw
the morning light glaze the door jamb.
I'm so high I can pass verdict on the birds.
Oh, can I be seen? In this high room,
I'm balanced as if it's a branch.

The city is purring its blood along 74th.
Central Park is a bright green page corner
turned over, in the distance. Can I find
my place again? I turn to yesterday
afternoon – I need to cool down, it feels
like I've been taken with fever. *Consider
the lilies of the field* and me unclothed.

The watering accounts

The earth was too dry, water runs straight through the chilli-seed pots, water needs a little of itself to be charmed.

I discover a brimstone butterfly folded between the indoor plant pots like a brief handwritten letter, full of information from the nectar-wet sex of flowers, a butterfly made of yellow silk-dust from a bedroom stool, the colour of a post-it left on the window sill fading all year, found, in a spring clean, now barely legible save one black full stop, a beauty spot on each papery cheek.

The big metal watering can with hinged handle, swaying, metal meeting water, a high cough in an echo chamber, the sound of canal arch.

Some leaves are haired but the cucumber leaf is furry, and ragged as fighting dogs' ears, the water sits up miraculously balled on its raised hairs, they're goose bumps on a man's arm in summer rain, sure rooves sloping protection for baby cucumbers slung sleeping below.

Distracted by weeding, once again I left the watering can filling from the butt, the gravel flooded – a libation.

The basil seedlings are deceptive, the soil looks damp when bone dry, water consumption is way out of kilter for the size, they don't like the plastic pots and fade, those in the clay pots surge forward, leggy like young race horses; bolting.

Some days the watering takes half the day – break – pour water from the filter to the kettle then into the teapot, into the cup, to my mouth. Then it rains. It pours.

Angela once said that parenting is immersive

We are paddling in a splash of children when Sarah
holds up a wet stone, it's the shape of a breast: *symbol
of my parenting life,* she says. The sphere was the tint
and opacity of cold, stewed tea: the thing was tannin
strong. It's not hot-swollen nor punctured flat but the size
of a small, clenched fist, perfectly hard and round except
drawn to a neat bifurcated pout. *It's even got a cracked
nipple,* I point out. In the cliff car park by the gritty
toilets with no mirrors, on a *What did you find today?*
ID board, a *mammoth tooth, anemone fossil* and there,
unmistakable, her stone, named as *cannon shot flint*—
a cup of boiling quartz cooled to indestructible grace.

Documentary

Last night I was watching a documentary about the photographer Juergen Teller and cutting off my cuticles. Both lasted the same time: I should say I slipped with the cuticle tool and cut too deeply into my left thumb, which bled. I put my son to bed; he wrapped his arms around me, patted my shoulder tenderly then pinched my nose hard and asked if it hurt. I went downstairs to feed the washing machine again, made a hot honey and lemon drink though I probably didn't need it and was reminded of a poem about squeezing a lemon for a head cold, that was also about the knots we tie in love and loss, by which we are undone, and the moments when this is not at all OK. Then the fruit bowl glowed. Perhaps because I was wearing my reading glasses, two red-striped apples, side-by-side, caught my eye. The dried-up old petals on the bottom of the apples fluttered like lashes; thick, twisted, cartoon-lashes and the right-hand apple winked.

I keep a Kilner jar of sea shells on the shelf,

the salty preservation
of one unmemorised day,
drowning steeped in broken
open sea, bottled

ozone waves unbolting,
a half of hand-pulled
rockpool, glass, cool as
the North Sea. Sifting

sound as the jar lid
surfs off. I hold the foam
in my lap, lap up
the rotten dead-gull smell;

do cockles and whelks
birth their young inside
their shells, dream their
corrugated mathematics?

Post-diluvial interview

no one knew why /
and it was relentless /
breaking all records until
records didn't exist /
we lived lashed together / boats
laced close like lover's fingers /
to make an island / off no land /
untethered to the dead /
we didn't call it rain
we called it *unlucky* and *because* / like it was
a bad dog / we harnessed it / wrought arrays
of tiny water wheels to power trembling light and heat /
so — what would you miss? only the fish survived with us
and other multiplicities of sea creatures / small details /
the intimate details / I know you want to know /
how do people live in extremis? Berber Inuit Nenet /
in the belly of the sleeping boats /
some slept in for days / we ate details of details /
things that moved / flying dying insects seaweed
our own soft fingernails /
couples took honeymoons from the compression /
you know / the buoyant company of what was left /
in holiday caves of diminishing phallic peaks
they always returned with an undercooked look / raw as meat /
remember / their skin just couldn't cope /
what I craved / the only quiet place
away from the crying assembly line of the rain /
ironically was the underwater / a huge risk / to unclip / sink
unexpectedly / fill like cloud / sculling the fins of my skirt /
as the sea diluted / salt became a problem
friends often licked each other clean /
for the fringe benefits and not to waste a thing /
I started a cottage industry weaving and knitting
ripped up strips of plastic bags for capes and hoods /
harvested / as we did everything from the filter of chafing hulls /
the *grimace* the in-between / salvage

was a precious finite resource of course /
I had started to wonder / was it only a matter of time
before we would not be able
to return to the dry /
why it stopped /
no one knew

Glass mariner

you look lost / she says to me / but vertebrae know the way /
climb us up in the halflight / slop / slop of cerebrospinal seas /
and it is very cold down here / the concrete steps ring hollow
submarine-y sounds / round and round / bare as a wrecked
whelk-shell / its wall beaten away by waves / only the spiral
stairwell is retained / in case you're interested / I've just noticed
our guide is a convalescent ghost /
Grace says / *at my core I'm*
ice-cream and storm / clean as a whistle I pass right through her /
glassy / her voice continues / *the pockmarks on the concrete*
are... / I think she is saying this inside my head / *not unlike*
the bubbles of breath caught in antique glass / she never did
really get warm again after that wretched night at sea /
Grace says /
I didn't save them all you know / I nod / I stand there / dripping
unaccountably / what can we say / about the vortex of water /
you are sucked down / below hypothermic marination / **Grace**
says / with a gleam / *in the lantern room I'll graffiti our names*
on the window with my engagement ring / *to mark the occasion* /
I witness the words materialising across the lighthouse glass
like little sticky cyanotic fingerprints / in squint lines / kneading
the surface of the sea / through the double-glazed panes / I'm /
pleading for oblivion of sunlight /
over the lantern room /

catcall gulls bombing oily white paint on black rocks / blue plaster
eroded to cloudy grey patches as if to camouflage us inside sky /
the fleet of sea birds boomerang on air-swells / fly into their own
reflections / this glass drum beats out regular light / blinks hope /
and Hail Marys / this window frame chops up the sea into
manageable pieces / a search and rescue grid / Great Black Backs
stamp and herd on the skyroof / drop of blood red on the bill
to show their intent / for those in peril / variegated in winter
plumage / the sea / is a riff on drunken flints / *nearer to sentient ice*
it was that night / *wet fingers* /
Grace says / *my oars my arms*
my back weighing out stones / *over and over* /
the over there
is always hanging on the horizon / slow motion by distance /
an apparition / subdued on vertical and horizontal planes /
a cormorant draughts its line straight as a skimming stone /
Grace says / *as air moves across the turbine* / *the blades make*
the hub rotate / she says it is a long way down through cold cloud

Blessèd

wave-angel
strange rainbow
aspirational avian
an inverted dive
by fluted fan-fin
fish out of water
outboard-racer
wet-needle
harpoon-snout
half-mast
amphibic aplomb
surf-plough
sea-stitch
air-risker
convertible
not fish nor fowl
helium-ish
scene-stealer
breath-taking
fabulous mythical
made-to-measure creature
in couture wings
Patron-Saint-
of-the-in-between
flight-of-undiluted-
self-belief
salted magic
flying fish

iii. sons of sons

In Bamford churchyard at 5 o'clock we hold hands.

We bridge the freshly mounded earth to lift the lilies off the grave first: fragile as they are, they surprise us with a small dead weight, we try hard not to wake them, slumped on greenstick wrists, resting their drowsy heads on praying leaves. In the lee of the valley, with views down and beyond the sheep field, from under the apple tree, I think this really is the perfect spot to lie in long grass, listen to the church bells singing. We plant our three-year-old's poster-paint handprints in the clay soil; daubs of orange and yellow, not too deep, like bulbs for spring. We water them with tears. The boy wanders off; is swallowed by the late October afternoon tucking dusk in, around the headstones. I think of sons of sons. I think about the little hands we bury here today and their quick fingers rooting down through the soil to find his grandfather's creased cheek; investigate his stubble chin, hold his hand, accompany him.

Ladybower

That I could give him back to you, so you would
find him in your wardrobe warming his tweed

jacket, blowing his nose on a fresh handkerchief
from your drawer, you would see him as geometry:

a straight line in the ghost shadows. If the folded
sheet of cloud laid out across this watery sky

could release him, in a shower of small parts,
as something we could piece together between us,

like a jigsaw. I should have gone to see his body.
The living, all vertical as the dam walls, absorbing

the light like summer leaves in tall beech woods.
He lay uncovered; milk turning in the parlour.

Out in the afternoon darkness, the valley hardly
able to bear the huge weight of the reservoir,

gold leaves are spinning on the surface: its black
depths poured into another glass of tap water.

Lichen!

you are minuscule   beneath arboreal breath   you are in veins

of stone in a loop   thrills of orange   splats of acid lemon

you are a *both*   you append as agenda carbon-forged corsage

barometer of health   you are a canary   expand infinitesimally

hush-hush in plain sight   become tangible   inhabit each other

corporeal wall   you say this say that   say you live on concrete pill-box

slumped on sandy heath   overlooking the sea   say you can remember

snaked razor wire   squadrons of sirens   hurling the smell of fear

into the grain of old men   the biding of women   you say this wall is mine/ours

fluoroscrawl here I am/ here   we are mutualism   in bloom

If I were to land

as a woodcock, in your hands,
rescued from the street and be offered to you,
suppose by a passer-by who might have considered,
that with your feathery face and egg-blue eyes
you seemed like someone who would know what to do
with a broken bird, with a bloody nose, two miniature
tears, dripping scarlet as a pierced heart would
in a painted manuscript, then if you assembled
a cage of ribs, lined it with hair from your own brush
and draped it with a sickbay hush, left me saucers
of water and worms, left the night to heal me and if I
dissolved as coloured light in rain, would you weep,
kneeling like a gilded saint, illuminated as you were,
when the rescued woodcock woke and walked
along the garden path, looked back twice then flew

A Pre-Columbian figure in and out of the house of Frida Kahlo

Teotihuacan boy you're ousted from the belly of the world and its border palaces
of Sun and Moon. Pequeño crescent nose, scrap of chin, elbows stuck in place

are set forever on your knees and packed in straw, five centimetres
of rare clay, small as a hand-warmer, hardly holding on to the marketplace

heat, smelling of hot, red plain. You were delivered, late in the afternoon,
tan like dry avocado seed: a homecoming the painter couldn't even place

in her lap, another delicate injury. Did you sleep in the man's truck,
in a hoard, in the black skull of a frog pot, find your toes a safe place

to rest on the lip of a cup: dream a past life of procession, rigmarole
and birdheads, laden temples on the Avenue of the Dead and gold place-

settings? A new wind blew in a climate unkind to pear-shaped things.
But this is quite a different suburb: to sit on Frida's ziggurat fireplace,

by the terracotta chimney on Colonia del Carmen as crowds filter through
the Blue House; to stare into the museum of Frida's body, stand in her place.

Away north, another line, another truck to the fence, trial by desert or freeway
beyond the U.S. border. One boy is processed; the next boy takes his place.

Nativity at night

Hundreds of hours away across motorway tracts
and sleeping tarmac fields, over the static-hiss haloing
plastic logistics barns to a room, unlit as the garden shed,
its dark night compressed into an ebony dice, where
another diminutive barely-balanced as an ounce of cornflour
is pale in adoration by quiet fire; you see him alight,
alive in your mind, through glass-thin skin his perilous
newborn warmth, the afterglow of an incandescent bulb.

She has not yet thought the thought

I cannot live without him

First standing. Now on her knees, on a field of stones.
She is a grounded boat. His skin is scored until it flaps,
frays then peels off like a seared fish. Onto her lap
he's slung. She holds this flinty pity close as bones.

> *slippery as first breath, light*
> *as a blown egg he is empty as a cup*

This body lies here chill and green, an olive in the jar,
wasted as the oil that feeds the dust when the jar dropped.
Unfriendly lamp in a hollow night. We all tremble like a flock
before dawn. Oh and yes – he was frightened of the dark.

> *hang my skin to dry over the funeral fire*
> *to make a decent coat*

To start with, can you carve a man out of words
(or want) as he would make a steady bench, firm door,
a floor, a plate, twelve faithful chairs, a willing table or
a hook, on which to hang the thread of what was heard?

> *they are saying they have touched his side,*
> *his inside, seen him – with their eyes*

The pointless cave yawns. Another bored stone basks
in the exclamations over the fruitless drone of sunrise flies.
It's still cold as mud in here and worse than occupied.
Shrill myrrh remains but there's no bad meat to mask.

> *I will climb the tree of him, the trunk*
> *and limb, to see if I can see his body coming*

Her ankle turns on loose grit. For three nights unslept,
now she's clumsy with hurry and slips in goat shit,
searching for any signs of him; a shivering lizard whips
his hem through the dust, she hears his equal step.

> *silent in the air, I'll move me*
> *like smoke, ahead of any wheel*

Mary unwraps his tools, holds the adze, the chisel.
Her night and day are bitten down in keeping watch
from a window that cannot rest; the door is unlocked
and it fidgets in the wind. She is ready as a well.

> *mountains like Romans are storming*
> *the house, the sun is burning open*

his flight eclipsed, only Icarus
    notices the sawn waves of liquid flint,
their chalky white edge, the frilled blade,
    a wave, an apparition of infinity,
the incomplete globe swiftly approaches
    and how imperfect that cold hole
which he unscrews headfirst
    into abysmal sea, O FATHER,
Icarus is an iron hammer slamming
    down though air, he notices his muscle
made hot metal to the anvil sea,
    sea-wrought cells rewritten, he knows
saltwater boils when it quenches his
    capsized human shape polished
in the cast of sea void and slowly
    sunk, the rush and muzzled sound
of impact, the feathered wreckage
    in a puckered drawstring trough contracts;
from above, the body of a bird
    drowning, a complacent surface

Lifeboat men
from the Book of Lists

can you see them, in concentric circles around the eyehole of Tom 'Barnes'
Cooper's copper-coloured telescope, the way ripples persist after
something's lost on an open and infinite sea? What this glass eye has seen!
Whose sandpaper hands worked wear into the tanned leather? A little
gloss, lick and spit of saline sheen, still doggedly clings to the barrel.

OLD JOHN TAR BISHOP
OLD JON CASKE
TIPPOO COOPER
TOM BARNES COOPER
COCKNEY COX
CRIB CRASKE
DINGEY CRASKE
OGLESS FARROW
SALTER FARROW
JOCKEY GRIMES
SAFFRON GRIMES
BUTTER BOLLS GRICE
KING KONG GRICE
LOLLY GRICE
BELCHER JOHNSON
BUTCHER JOHNSON
KIFFER JOHNSON
MAGGOT JOHNSON
OLD SKYE JOHNSON
READY JOHNSON
SPIDER JOHNSON
UNCLE JOHNSON
JOHN LONG
OLD ROOK REYNOLDS
DICK TWIRL
SQUINTER WEST

Boy

His hands are two small birds.

Still unwrought, untempered,
marshmallow flesh over pliant bone.

When they cover his face, I break.

As they ripen,
they try on the adult language
of gesture, like new white gloves.

This poems takes 82 seconds

*At 2.40pm on 17th March 2017 a terrorist attack
took place on Westminster Bridge: 4 died and 50
were injured including three teenagers in a French
school group.*

the French boy is talking again   on the radio   I feel the hush of us all   listening
    inside eyes adrift   I know Westminster   the Thames   who doesn't   the Bridge
its jammed pavements   sticky vortex of lurching red and camera lenses   the French boy
  is talking again   but all the vital detail is added by the interviewer   stage directions
   when and then   it's impossible for the French boy   as none of this is making any sense
I lie wholly quiet   as a letter in an envelope   listen to the radio   picture my husband
  running wide open   his flashing legs   scissored silver light on crumpled water
still warm places   remain under the covers of the bed   the French boy is talking again
  cannot explain   did the car mount the pavement and did the air explode   last night
I curled around my boy   an avocado around its stone   I really want the interview to end
  a bough at the window   a crisp green stem   waiting   nothing cannot be said
  translations don't add back up   the sound   of his breath   between words   accruing

Strawberry jam

This. This is the spot. This is where I would have been left behind
if I had been left behind but I haven't this is where I'll be
ploughed under, I thought, useful fruit at least.

Until you came along. I'm blinded, you see, but I can hear you...
blurred. Nothing is clear. *Oo swee-je? Where am I?* – they taught us
that at least. I can't really see. That's where, here, gassed.

Khaki, cack, mire, sludge, slurry, slashing up hell's rain from
the ground, like the horse pissing in your eye that time. I'd eat anything
but I'm not hungry. *Non, no. I said.* The front takes everything –

including your appetite, bon appétit to you though, I know that one,
white bread tearing, I can hear it, I can smell it. We only get
plum jam. Have you got strawberry? Strawberry jam,

are they picking? We'd be picking now or just about, just about.
Warm strawberries in the bloody burning sun. I thought I hated
picking them, kneeling in the field between the rows, rotten fruit

giving way under the weight, to rancid pulp, stooped all day. Mud
soup, craters of mud soup filling your eyes, bowls and bowls, *hot soup*
all round when you get back lads they didn't say. I shouldn't

have been left behind, there's the line of black trees, I think I can see
our scrambling hedge, our gate at home. Water? a nice long drink, yes,
yes I have a thirst, thank you – I thank you, mercy.

Codes of conduct

On manoeuvres:

A polestar torch sparks up. The profile of the black pine solidifies into a guardian,
a protector of shrinking light. Bats, half-moth half-lark, their shoulders hunched,
are rowing the night, for their lives. Their film is speeded up: they translate the ghastly
slow motion as *Avoid!* The breaking news like birdsong calling all the violet night long.

> *So much happened in a day*
> *and I must say all of this*
> *in case I do not wake*

In the training camp:

Overlit and urbane under spotlights at The Barracks,
this pair are blinded under their blinkers, sheathed

softly and half-cocked. A couple of satyr twins
are running toward the sun. Even at noon, they waltz

the muggy darkness found in the upper part
of the skull and then, gingerly, rag-bind

their scarred thighs, jog on the spot, slap knees, slay
Greek-Gods style. How long have they champed

and pawed like this, the sterile air of heaven,
clutching their arguments? Who but they would wear

their lungs on the outside like a jumper, a waistcoat,
a lifejacket, play blind man's buff in skin jodhpurs?

Here is now. When gods fall to earth. Second division
deities scythed from a mind's eye into the fact

of senses. There is a horsey smell, stringy limbs,
exo-skull, a jockstrap, finely worked sage-coloured

metal – soft, leafy bronze armour. The rub, the blister,
the chafe. Hardware congealing in skin. Recognise them

as puppets pulling their own strings. It's futile;
they are tied now to the earth with their own

impossible weight: thwarted hot air balloons,
their hubris renders them impotent. Unlaunched.

They remain explaining to themselves: this training
camp, this tortured circle reductive as dressage.

> *In here we are all prisoners of the war*
> *I will obey the lawful*
> *I will give no information*

The Nerve Centre:

A Brylcreemed cry, a squadron of oiled crows
arranged on the lawn in a geometry of fear. Discipline.

The prisoner's rebel head is marked in quadrants
like a butcher's diagram of a side of beef.

Orbit his pocked skin, it's leathery under the sheen,
in the wet emulsion of basement window-light and filth,

past his unmoved eyes, drawn down to the left, waiting
to replay the story, an old black-and-white film, memory

on the screen of the floor. The scars are where
they said they would carve him, find their answers

written on his skull. How much can a body endure?
Pain is ice white; pain is a universal space and he is lost

like an astronaut   jettisoned

                              is falling through

                  is wrought in their hotwork
                              of words and shoulder blades

hooded, walled, four days standing on a cardboard box

filled with saltwater like a bucket

                  he is raw fumbling in space dust, dark matter
            in the threadbare cloth of culture

They are in dialogue. Their amputated dialogues.

                              I will never forget the knife is a hand's extension
                              licked for the taste of danger
                              liked for its sweet tip

The Un-Hurting Room:

From down the corridor you hear the squawking.
The men have taken off their heads, and for the time being,

stored them neatly as helmets in The Armoury
on breeze-block plinths. What a relief (they can be heard

thinking) to unburden ourselves. De-baggage.
Little songs of birds fly out half-smiling, they call

and chatter like teeth. Gogglehead Goggleheads
Goggled head *One, two. By the left, quiiick*

march! two three. What is it to congregate, to pack,
to animal? Intoxicating. My God, they believe

in this! The clouds run backwards. The gulls keep calling,
wading through burn-bag scraps at the council dump.

This is down time. Dorm time. Porn time.
One steps out for a smoke. Takes off his gold neck chain,

its pure line becomes corrupted, pile-up the chain-links,
pile them up like other men, like sandbags

in the exercise yard. When a chain is abandoned to mess –
becomes knotted, was once valuable, like honour

and its friend loyalty – it cannot be undone. The seagulls
seen at dawn flock in the blue dusk about to be shattered.

> *If I become a prisoner of any war*
> *I will keep faith*
> *with my fellow prisoners*

In the Major's Room:

Gods and dogs. What would his mother say? His head in his hands, elbows
on the desk, in the half-dark the Major remembers this (to forget himself) –

the Birdman of Liverpool, Leo Valentin... it is 1957, his flight
falters, he falls through self-conviction into death in front
of 100,000... how I watch in expectation, the warrior's head
had fallen... *and pity... pity,* I hear mother say holding
my hand very tightly, Birdman's blood just ink leaking
into newsprint, men's hands attempt to cup the swollen head;
hands, making a nest for a huge swollen egg, a gift ungiven.

I will never forget
I am responsible for my actions
I was brave though

The Ante-Room:

In the adjacent locker room, tin wardrobes
are stockpiled with ears, pegged onto coat hangers,

lined up. Cooperation. The ears are talking.
To each other. *If you listen, you cannot speak.*

Any counsel falls on deaf ears, no one knows why
they are here. Imprisoned, as condemned by repetition

as Echo and Narcissus, like a crack habit,
as Prometheus' liver was picked at and grew back.

Forever is a long long time. Under the heavy metal
armour, throbbing cells persist, squeezing the heart,

flesh doors flap, wave blood through like traffic police
at a road accident. The Uniform is flagging.

And afterwards, to soothe their aching backs,
a communal bath, sliced-up sun-warm oranges, a teat

of ewe's milk, bread and olives; after the payback,
after the good beating that they gave out, this bliss

of clean righteousness, buoyed up, floating on
your brother's watered-down blood, your cousin's

second-hand dirt, their epithelium avascular but
innervated. After all is said and done it comes

back to the body. See Christ packed into the tomb,
the nailed crate, in Holbein's claustrophobia

of proximal enclosure, half dead, half living, eyes
open, mouth open, the winding sheet. How tender

each cell: each has its work, first to sense then repair,
prevent abrasion, desiccation, invasion, trauma.

It could be any body. Smell his rotting greenish flesh,
the body being hurt, injury after injury.

> *I will take command*
> *I will take no part in any action*
> *which might be harmful*

The Ossuary:

You come across it, stacked
with salt-white bones of other

men, in a beach tomb of sand cliffs; The 'Geometry of fear' was an
informal group of sculptors, named by Herbert Read, working after the
Second World War.

a landslide had left a room with bare-root
roof, still abundant cedar needles spiked the air
sweet with green incense, to consecrate sea wind.

> *The light flickered when I turned away*
> *when I looked back it steadied*
> *under my gaze.*

The dead's prayer for the living:

                    You are forgiven your deserted lips, your

          unsurpassable,

temperate cave. You are forgiven your filth. You are forgiven

      your spine and mutability, the simplification

                in the codes of chivalry. You are forgiven

your calcification. If you forgive ours.

      To forgive, like any

          contract, something must

                        be given.

Notes

twelve impossible things
The phrases in italics are 'found' text gathered from various well intentioned on-line guides to coping with infertility.

'the camera is an instrument'
Dorothea Lange was an American documentary photographer and photojournalist, she worked for the Farm Security Administration (FSA) in the 1930's to record the rural poverty of migrant farm workers and Dustbowl refugees during the Great Depression in the United States. The photograph referred to is 'Migrant Mother'.

Diptych
The left part Anne. refers to Anne Boleyn 150(1)7 -1536 born at Blickling Hall, Norfolk and right part Elizabeth. 1533 - 1603 to her daughter Elizabeth I.

Glass Mariner
The daughter of a lighthouse keeper, Grace Darling became a national heroine. She risked her life rowing single-handed in a ferocious storm to rescue stranded survivors of the steamship 'Forfarshire' wrecked off the Northumberland coast in 1838. She died died 4 years later, aged 26, from tuberculosis reportedly having never been fully well since that night.

Lifeboat men
Tom 'Barnes' Cooper's copper-coloured telescope can be seen in the collection in Sheringham Museum amongst photographs and other objects related to heroic lifeboat operations. It can been seen from the names how the crewing duties ran in families.

This poem takes 82 seconds
At 2.40pm on 17th March 2017 a terrorist attack took place on Westminster Bridge, London: four died and 50 were injured including three teenagers in a French school group.

Codes of Conduct
This poem was sparked by notes made in the exhibition Elisabeth Frink: Humans and Other Animals at Sainsbury Centre for Visual Arts, Norwich, 2018. The italicised lines are based on 'found' text from U.S. military 'codes of conduct' articles. The 'Geometry of fear' was an informal group of sculptors, named by Herbert Read, working after the Second World War.